a smart girl's guide

Digital World

how to connect, share, play, and keep yourself safe

by Carrie Anton
illustrated by Stevie Lewis

Published by American Girl Publishing

No part of this book may be used or reproduced in any manner whatsoever without written permission except in the case of brief quotations embodied in critical articles and reviews.

17 18 19 20 21 22 23 QP 10 9 8 7 6 5 4 3 2 1

Editorial Development: Darcie Johnston
Art Direction and Design: Jessica Rogers
Illustrations: Stevie Lewis
Production: Jeannette Bailey, Caryl Boyer, Cynthia Stiles, Kristi Tabrizi

The Consultants

Megan A. Moreno, MD, MSEd, MPH, is a pediatrician and the principal investigator of the Social Media and Adolescent Health Research Team in the Center for Child Health, Behavior and Development, Seattle Children's Research Institute.
Jane Annunziata, PsyD, is a clinical psychologist specializing in children and families, and the author of many mental health and wellness books for children.

Library of Congress Cataloging-in-Publication Data

Names: Anton, Carrie, 1977- author. | Lewis, Stevie, illustrator.
Title: A smart girl's guide : digital world : how to connect, share, play, and keep
    yourself safe / by Carrie Anton ; illustrated by Stevie Lewis.
Description: Middleton, WI : American Girl, 2017.
Identifiers: LCCN 2016044647 (print) | LCCN 2016045817 (ebook) |
    ISBN 9781683370437 (pbk.) | ISBN 9781683370420 (ebook)
Subjects: LCSH: Internet and children—Juvenile literature. | Internet—Safety measures—
    Juvenile literature. | Online social networks—Safety measures—Juvenile literature. |
    Privacy, Right of—Juvenile literature. | Girls—Conduct of life—Juvenile literature.
Classification: LCC HQ784.I58 A58 2017 (print) | LCC HQ784.I58 (ebook) |
    DDC 004.67/8083—dc23
LC record available at https://lccn.loc.gov/2016044647

americangirl.com/service

As you use apps, games, e-mail, websites, and new technologies still waiting to be invented, you'll get more comfortable—and smarter—with your virtual habits and preferences.

Your personality online may be a bit different from your personality when you meet face-to-face with people. That's not because you're being fake. It's because you might respond differently to digital interactions. Maybe you're shy in class or with other groups, for instance, but online you find more space and time to think. And typing out words on a screen might be more in your comfort zone than having all eyes on you while you talk.

In the digital world, as in real life, the possibilities are whatever you want them to be. Find your favorite ways to express your ideas, keep yourself safe . . .

and stay true to the real you.

Do you have a technology tale to tell?

Write to us!
Digital World Editor
American Girl
8400 Fairway Place
Middleton, WI 53562

Here are some other American Girl books you might like:

Each sold separately. Find more books online at americangirl.com.

contents

Dear Reader,

Technology makes life so much easier! No more getting lost, thanks to map apps. A face-to-face talk with your favorite aunt who lives on the other side of the world can take place right on your screen. When a word trips you up while you're reading, the definition is a tap away in your e-book. And that's just for starters. The truth is, digital technology is changing the way we live every day, in almost every way.

Even with all the benefits, though, the online world can be tricky to navigate. Just like when you're riding a bicycle, you need to know the risks and the rules for staying safe. Life in the digital sphere also means making decisions about how you present yourself every time you go there. You might even feel like you're living two different versions of yourself: the real you and the virtual you.

This book shows you how to be true to the real you, how to take care of yourself, and how to make the most of digital technology. Advice from real girls will help you use this technology without getting sucked into drama. Quizzes will test your online safety smarts. You'll discover ways that tech can help you manage things like schoolwork. And best of all, you'll find tons of ideas for connecting with friends, family, classmates, and other citizens of the digital world.

Ready to sign on?

Your friends at American Girl

daily devices

I love the Internet world! I love to make videos of crafts and e-mail pictures of my dogs and share information and ideas that people may use in their actual life!

—Lisa

SAFETY MATTERS

Learning how to navigate the digital world requires a coach. Some sites are made for girls your age, but many are not. Your age determines the social media sites that are right for you. Always go online with your parent until you have permission to go alone, and always comply with the terms and conditions of any website you visit.

gadget girl

Once upon a time, a school essay had to be tapped out on a typewriter instead of a keyboard. A rented movie was a tape that said "Be kind, rewind!" on the case. If you missed an episode of your favorite TV show, you could only hope to see it the next summer, when the channel showed it again. Games mostly came in boxes. Birthday cards only came in paper envelopes. The telephone was attached to a wall!

Today, all those things have changed because of gadgets that make life faster and easier than ever before—gadgets that put a whole world at a girl's fingertips. These gadgets are changing how we work and play in ways that we never could have imagined only a few years ago.

Today, it's a snap to . . .

do research for school.

play a game—solo.

take a pic—
with besties.

make a
movie.

8

listen to tunes—
wherever.

stream a TV show—
whenever.

read your
favorite book.

learn something new.

communication scene

Gadgets are changing how we do things, but that's not all. They're also changing how we express ourselves and spend time together. Words like *friend* and *chat* have whole new meanings in the digital world. Words like *blog* and *e-mail* have been created to name technologies as they've been invented. A girl can shine on the online stage in many more ways than before, but the technologies and sites you can use depend on how old you are.

Type a text

Stay in touch with quick messages to friends and family.

Send an e-mail

For short messages, texting is great. But to really connect, type and send a letter-like e-mail—with pictures—to a friend or family member.

Chat via video

Too far away to meet in person? Turn a face-to-face convo into a screen-to-screen chat.

Share something

With the OK from your parents, write a post, take a pic, or shoot a video, and share it with your friends using an app added to your device.

Blog about it

A blog is like an online journal that you give permission to certain people (such as your family) to read. With help from a parent, write posts about a project you're researching or a good cause you're supporting.

Run for the world!

Launch an IM

Want to get a group chat going? Invite your friends, classmates, or family members to an instant-message group.

connected classroom

If you've ever searched online for Rosa Parks facts for social studies, prepped for a multiplication test using an online math game, or set up your erupting-volcano science fair project with tips from an online tutorial, then you already know there's tons to learn in the digital world. As you work your way to the head of the class, these other ways of tapping into technology can also help you make the grade.

Teacher time

Home sick from school? To get assignments and materials, check in with teachers on their websites or by sending e-mails. You don't have to fall behind when a bug's got you down.

Classy computers

Computers and digital devices are go-to places for info, just like the classroom and library bookshelves. What's more, they can spice up a lesson with audio and video. Instead of photos in a textbook, imagine a time-lapse video of a caterpillar changing into a butterfly! Classroom tech can also get you learning with recording apps, interactive whiteboards, and slide shows produced by *you*.

Digital study buddy

During at-home study time, send a group e-mail or start a closed chat page. It's easy to connect with other students in your class when you need help with an assignment or just want to test one another on the state capitals and spelling word list.

Search-and-click resources

In addition to books and magazines, your library may have special search engines for students, online encyclopedias and databases, and homework-helping software when you need to write a report or prep for a quiz.

Group project

Finding a time for everyone to work on a group project can be tricky, especially when one person has soccer practice, one is babysitting, and one is at a chess tournament. Digital resources allow everyone to check in when they can using e-mail or text, and to work together using closed-group pages approved by teachers and parents.

digital mom and dad

When your parents were growing up, they didn't have most of the gadgets and apps you have today. But that doesn't mean they're living in the digital dark ages. In fact, they are using technology in lots of ways that you may not know about yet, but one day will. Here are just some of the ways they go digital to manage their lives—and yours.

shopping

working

paying bills

scheduling appointments

ordering pizza!

learning the ropes

Fun and games. School tools. Staying in touch. Managing life! With so much that's good about technology, is there a downside?

Technology can offer freedoms you don't find in the real world. But the freedom comes with responsibility, which means your parents need to assist for a while, until you learn the online ropes. It's not that they don't trust you. It's because online actions have consequences you may not know about.

The digital world is a big place. When you're texting a friend or posting a photo, literally anyone in the world might see—and it's easy to forget that some people online don't know you or care about you. Also, it's hard to imagine that what you do in the digital world stays forever. Once you've done it, you can't take it back—even if you wish you could.

Your parents will probably set rules, like which apps and websites you can visit, and with whom you can talk and share online. Think of it like learning an important skill, such as swimming, with a coach and lots of practice.

Start the conversation with your parents. Show them you're ready to be trusted to follow their digital rules. Suggest a contract, like the one here. The more open you are with your parents about your online life, the more likely they'll be to see you as a good digital citizen.

Digital World Contract

- ☐ I will not sign up for any site without my parents' OK.
- ☐ My parents and I will preview a site together before deciding to sign me up.
- ☐ My parents and I will register for my account and set privacy settings together, and I will not change any settings myself.
- ☐ My parents will have the usernames and passwords to any accounts I have.
- ☐ My parents will "friend" and "follow" me on all my sites and will be able to see everything I post.
- ☐ I will never post my last name, my home address, the name of my school, or other information that identifies me or my family—either in words or in pictures.

_____
Me

_____
Mom or Dad

play it safe

How I feel about the digital world is cautious. I'm careful to only share things with people I know and to keep my accounts private.

–Natalie

that's personal

No matter what digital stuff you do—play games, research homework, chat with friends, browse websites—the adults in your life will want to look over your shoulder and talk about safety. Why? you may wonder. You're not scaling ice-covered mountains. You're just hanging out at home, clicking and tapping. What harm could it do?

Lots, if you're not careful.

Public vs. private

Public means anyone can see. Websites and pages you find with a browser and without a password are public, including social media sites where people comment, play games, post photos, and share thoughts. *Private* means you control who can see what you do—or at least that's the idea. The truth is, nothing digital is ever completely private. E-mails and texts can be copied or forwarded to other people. Even posts in a social media account that you think are private can sometimes be tagged, shared, and copied.

Zipped lips and fingertips

Staying safe means using sites approved for your age. It also means thinking twice before you type or tap—no matter what age you are! To update an old-world phrase, safety is about keeping your digital lips zipped.

Sharing personal information can let a stranger know where you live, what school you go to, or the field where you play soccer. It can give bullies an opportunity to single you out. It can even allow someone to pretend to be you.

17

Know before you go

Before you go online to public or private websites, learn this list of important DON'Ts.

 Don't share digits. If it's got a number in it, keep it offline. That includes things like your address, birth date, age, phone number, and any account numbers.

 Don't give your name. It might be OK to use your first name if it's not unusual, but a nickname or online name is better.

Don't share selfies with people you don't know in your real life. Don't even use words to describe what you look like. People you know in real life already know about your green eyes or dark curly hair. There's no reason for anyone else to.

Don't give your location. In addition to your home, never share places where you often go, such as your school, a dance studio, the club where you volunteer, or a favorite hangout spot.

 Don't give personal information about your family and friends. Where your parents work, how much your brother makes in pizza delivery tips, or photos of your sister may not be personal to you, but those things are personal to them. When you're online, you're responsible for their safety and privacy as well as your own.

E-mail extras

E-mail is different from going online. But it's still a digital technology that works over the Internet, which means you still need to know how to play it safe.

Just like you do when you're online, keep numbers out of any digital correspondence—not just e-mail but also messages and texts.

Never send e-mails to strangers. And if you receive an e-mail from someone you don't know, don't respond—delete it.

Remember that anything you send can be sent to someone else (and someone else, and someone else, and . . .) without your knowing. Send with care!

When in doubt, hide out

Stay safe online by staying *anonymous*. That means keeping who you are, where you live, and where you go private. Except with e-mail, you can be anonymous online until you specifically tell or show who you are. It's like wearing an invisibility cloak, because other people see only . . .

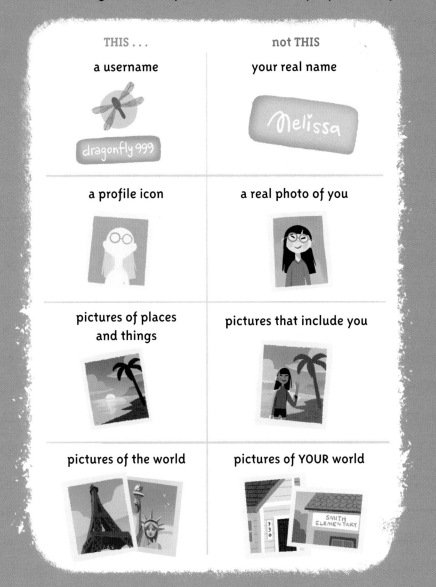

THIS . . .	not THIS
a username	your real name
dragonfly 999	Melissa
a profile icon	a real photo of you
pictures of places and things	pictures that include you
pictures of the world	pictures of YOUR world
	SMITH ELEMENTARY

Anonymous means . . .

talking about your hobbies, raving about your favorite bands, and liking other people's posts. You can do all these fun things without revealing your identity. But "anonymous" does *not* mean posing as someone else, either real or made-up. Giving false information about such things as your name, age, and physical description is potentially dangerous—and it's definitely off-limits.

getting connected

The digital world is like one of those cool old mansions filled with secret passageways and rooms. In the mansion, online accounts are like the light fixture you pull to reveal a hidden door. They're like the button you push to open a tunnel beneath a bookcase.

Anyone can roam through the public parts of the mansion with a search engine looking for things like videos about baby animals or a recipe for waffle-cone s'mores. But only your own (or your parents') personal account can get you into the following specific places and experiences:

e-mail

digital music library

online games

movie and TV streaming

virtual clubs

photo-sharing sites

age-appropriate social media

Key to accounts

Parents hold the keys to unlocking all those secret passageways and hidden rooms. Without their permission, most online places are off-limits because of age restrictions, because they cost money, or for the sake of safety.

If your parents give you any digital keys, remember that they come with responsibility. When you use a personal account, always remember:

Log in to start, and log out to end. Just as you wouldn't leave the door to your house open, don't leave your accounts open either. This is especially important when using public WiFi or public computers, such as at school or in the library.

Don't share personal information. Online accounts connect you with other people, some of whom you don't know well, if at all. Remember that personal info should always stay private.

Make sure your parents have your passwords. Your mom or dad won't be worried about the "Purr-fect Cat Plays with Yarn Ball" video you're sharing with your bestie, but they do want to check in to make sure you're safe.

what's the password?

•••••••••

Any time you set up an online account, you need to create a password. The password you pick should be something you can remember or keep track of, because you'll use it every time you log in. On the other hand, it shouldn't be one that someone else can figure out. That means . . .

 Skip names. Your name—as well as pet, family, friend, and even school names—can be easy for others to decode.

Forget your birthday. Since lots of people besides you know this info, it doesn't make a good password.

Nix the example. Don't choose a password that's used as an example. "Password1234" is often shown as an example for a site, but it isn't meant to protect your account.

Avoid personal information. Addresses, phone numbers, and e-mail addresses are things that make it easy for other people to identify you.

⚠ **Warning! Not for friends**

Passwords are like any other secret. If you share them with even one friend, they can make their way to other people. Your parents are the only people who should know your passwords. If you think a friend has the scoop on your secret code, create a new password to keep your accounts secure.

Password prompts

Feeling stumped? Fill in the prompts below (leaving out any spaces), and you'll create a password that's sure to secure your account but silly enough to stick in your noggin!

petunia + 99 + Gray = petunia99Gray

a summer flower | your favorite number, twice | the color you like least, capitalized

Autumn + 3 + AQ = Autumn3AQ

your favorite season, capitalized | the number of states you've lived in | your bestie's initials in reverse order

8 + effarig + ? = 8effarig?

the number of girls in your math class | your favorite zoo animal, spelled backward | one of these symbols: # * ! ? &

june + 13 + Hazel = june13Hazel

the month your mom was born | the year you started kindergarten | your dad's eye color, capitalized

eye + * + Pepperoni + 2 = eye*Pepperoni2

a body part | one of these symbols: # * ! ? & | your favorite pizza topping, capitalized | the number of floors in your school

potter + 333 + Story = potter333Story

the second word of your favorite book title | the number of sneaker pairs you own, three times | the last word of your fave movie title, capitalized

Be different

Be ultra safe and smart by giving every account a different password. That way, if someone decodes one, they don't have access to all of your accounts. If you're afraid you can't keep track of them all, ask your parents about a password manager program that saves them for you.

danger zone

You don't ride a bike without a helmet or walk down a dark street alone. The dangers are obvious. But when you're online, it's not so easy to see them.

1. This e-mail comes to your inbox. Would you respond or ignore?

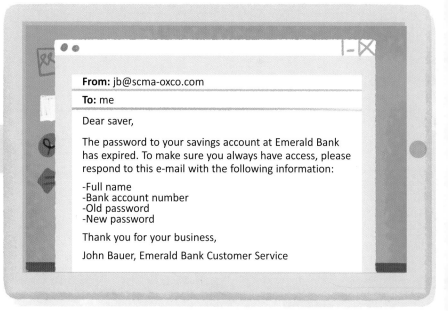

From: jb@scma-oxco.com

To: me

Dear saver,

The password to your savings account at Emerald Bank has expired. To make sure you always have access, please respond to this e-mail with the following information:

-Full name
-Bank account number
-Old password
-New password

Thank you for your business,

John Bauer, Emerald Bank Customer Service

2. This ad pops up on your phone. Would you download or ignore?

Free music ringtones just a click away!

Download now to fill your phone with fun tunes.

3. *Ping!* You get this instant message. Would you click the link or ignore?

CALIFORNIA COAST

Hey friend,

Saw this awesome pic and it reminded me of you!

http://siteunknownZxz.code1.mal

Answers

If you answered **ignore** to all three, you're in the safe zone! Here are the dangers waiting to strike.

1. Phishing

Pronounced like "fishing," this scam uses e-mail messages to lure you into giving personal information. Phishing criminals are good at cheating people by sending e-mails that look like they come from a real place, like a bank or the government. Their goal is to get info about you that they can use to pretend to be you, and then get money in your name. This is called *identity theft*, and it can cause big problems for you and your family.

What to Do: To avoid these scams, never give personal info in an e-mail—not ever. Your parents can always contact the sender directly with a phone call or a letter to see if the request is real.

2. Malware downloads

Malware is a program that sneaks into a computer without you knowing it. It can be called a *virus*, because it's like an infection. It might also be called a *worm, scareware,* or another term, but its purpose is always the same: to damage your computer, secretly feed your personal information to identity thieves, or harm you in some other way. Malware can accidentally be downloaded from the Internet through pop-up ads, which are windows that suddenly appear when you're on a website.

What to Do: Always check with your parents before downloading anything to your computer, smartphone, or tablet. Also, ask your parents to show you how to close a pop-up ad in a safe way.

3. Malware links

Malware can get into your computer when you click on hyperlinks—or *links* for short. These bad links are everywhere in the digital world: in e-mails, texts, instant messages, social media posts, ads, and search results from your browser. Beware of any link, even if it comes from someone you know. That person's computer or gadget may be sending malware-infected messages without her knowing—which means her account or device has been broken into, or *hacked*.

What to Do: If a message from a friend seems weird or it just doesn't sound like her, don't click on any link in the message. Also, get in the habit of reading links for oddities such as small spelling changes. If there's any doubt, don't click or reply. Instead, send a separate message to the sender if you know her, and ask. Always ignore links from anyone you don't know.

set things straight

It's up to you not to give out personal info. But sometimes there's only so much you can do on your own to stay protected in the digital world.

Part of that is thanks to *cookies*. In digital-speak, these are not the chocolate-chip treats you dip in milk. When you visit websites, they often install cookies on your computer to follow your online moves. This is great when you want to remember places you visit regularly.

But not all digital cookies are good. Some create a record of you by tracking your online habits. Then they sell that info to advertisers and other companies. The good news is there are settings on computers and tech gadgets that can keep what you do under lock and key.

When your parents decide the level of security that's right for you and your family, you can help them with this list to beef up your settings.

 Adjust your browser. All browsers have a Preferences or Settings menu with privacy and security options. Online tutorials can help your parents figure out what's what.

Pop-not. Pop-ups can be turned off to prevent them from automatically coming up when you are online.

No thanks. If an app requests your permission to share data, select "no" or "never."

 Skip locations. Some gadgets and apps track locations. This should be turned off in the settings.

Stay private. Many accounts let users limit who can and can't see their activity. Accounts should be set up to keep you safe— but remember there's no such thing as complete privacy.

to be or not to be?

Going anonymous online can keep you safe. But the fun of connecting with friends and family means showing some of your real, personal life. When it comes to the two versions of you—**personal** or anonymous **profile**—do you know which one to use for each of these situations?

1. Sending your cousin a text with a link to a funny hot dog meme.

personal · profile

THEY CALL ME...

FRANK

2. Sending a get-well e-card to a friend using a website that requires creating an account.

personal · profile

3. Inviting someone you don't know to play chess using an app on your tablet.

personal · profile

4. Sending an e-mail to your teacher asking about a homework assignment.

personal · profile

5. E-mailing a selfie from your recital to a friend you met at dance camp last summer.

personal · profile

6. Submitting your poem for an online kids' poetry contest.

personal · profile

Answers

1. personal Your cousin is family, so it's OK that the information comes from your phone number. Text only with people you have met in real life and trust—never someone you only know online.

2. it depends! A parent will need to help you sign up for an account on the site, which may require personal information such as your name and an e-mail address. The good news is that your information is all behind the scenes. When sending the card, fill in the "From" name using just your first name or a username that your friend will recognize.

3. profile Social gaming apps and sites allow you to play games with people you don't know, so stay safe by playing undercover. If the game has an IM feature, ignore any messages and just focus on the game.

4. personal You and your teacher know each other, so it's safe to be you. Besides, she's not likely to respond if she doesn't know it's you!

5. personal It's been a while, so you may need to remind her that she knows you. E-mail is a pretty safe way to communicate with your real name, because e-mail accounts are private. But don't share other personal info in the words—or pictures—you send.

6. it depends! It depends on the kind of contest. Read the rules with your parents, and make sure it's OK to enter. If there's a prize, personal info might be requested. But if winning just means your poem will be published online, then use a profile or give only your first name and age without a picture or other identifying information.

Selfie smarts

It seems like *everyone* is popping up in pics, and you want in on the selfie fun. But you also know that staying safe is super important. Talk with your parents about rules that strike the right balance of keeping you safe while giving you face time online.

Know or no. Text or e-mail selfies only to people you know in person. For example, Grandma would totally love to see your brand-new set of sparkling braces.

Extra eyes. If posting pics online, make sure your parents can monitor your account.

Background check. Never let identifying info—ribbons you've won at school or your name spelled out in marquee letters on your wall—make its way into the frame.

Doubt it? If you're not sure a picture should be shared, don't!

screen queen

Being part of this digital world is awesome! One thing I especially love is that people can share their passions. I like to post inspirational quotes and educational articles about topics I'm interested in.

—Rachel

what you say matters

The digital world brims, bustles, and bristles with creativity, stories, and opinions. Millions of people are posting, commenting, sharing, and filling it with energy and personality every day. In the online world, everyone has a voice. Including you.

Have you gotten the thumbs-up from your parents? Do you know how to keep your safety and privacy Priority #1 by sharing from a protected profile? If your answers are *yes* and *yes*, you're ready to turn the number of people online from millions to millions-plus-one!

Post the write stuff

Do you have a way with words? Write on! Share your poems, short stories, chapters from your novel, craft instructions, or even just short thoughts. Type what you're thinking at the moment, or allow time for your ideas to deepen into something more creative.

Snap and send a pic

They say a picture is worth a thousand words, so just imagine how much you'd say if you shared a photo a day. Smartphones and tablets make snapping and sending pics easier than ever. When you're traveling with your family, playing with your puppy, or admiring the setting sun, capture the moment from behind the lens to share with friends and family.

Record and play

Have you dreamed of seeing yourself on the big screen? Get some practice on a smaller one by creating a video showcase of your mad ukulele skills, filming a stop-animation short using your dolls and stuffed animals, or teaching others how to make your famous cupcake frosting recipe.

Comment

Like having a conversation online, commenting on other people's posts, pics, and videos is a great way to show support for a friend or family member who is doing something cool online. It's also an easy way to ask questions with the goal of learning something new. So next time your bestie adds a short video of a dance she choreographed, cheer her on in the comments and ask if she can show you the steps at your next sleepover.

Share

If your friend ever ran for student council and asked you to pass out flyers, then you're already familiar with sharing. Online sharing happens when you send URL links through e-mails, texts, and comments to others who might be interested. Make sure links are safe before passing them on. Better yet, copy and paste them from websites yourself so you're not sharing unsafe sites by accident. So if Mom is training for a marathon, copy and paste a link from a website you found about energy-boosting running snacks. Or if Dad is always losing his keys, send him a safe link to a page filled with tips for locating misplaced objects.

finding your crowd

When you're in school, finding new friends could mean talking to the person who sits next to you in social studies, telling a joke to your seat buddy on the bus, sitting down at a new table in the lunchroom, or joining an after-school engineering club to meet people who love to build robots. With all of these people, it's easy to put a face to a name, know how they're feeling at the moment, and find out if they'd make good friends to hang out with on the weekends.

It's not so easy online. Despite all the friending, following, liking, and joining, it's difficult to know who you can really call your crowd. In fact, interacting with others can get pretty confusing when you take away the face-to-face part of communication.

If online friend-finding is tripping you up, think about what your virtual activity might look like in real life.

That vest is awesome!

Awesome vest!

There are lots of ways to find friends online. Start by looking for clues about things you might have in common, and post a comment letting the other person know you have similar interests. Unless you know this person in real life, you won't be as close as you would be with a friend from camp or band, for example. But it can be fun to know there are many people in the world with likes like your own.

emoji language

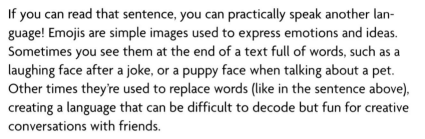*

If you can read that sentence, you can practically speak another language! Emojis are simple images used to express emotions and ideas. Sometimes you see them at the end of a text full of words, such as a laughing face after a joke, or a puppy face when talking about a pet. Other times they're used to replace words (like in the sentence above), creating a language that can be difficult to decode but fun for creative conversations with friends.

Emojis are a fun way to dress up your messages, but they can be troublemakers, too. There are thousands of emoji icons of faces alone—all with different expressions. Sometimes they're straightforward, such as a smiley or sad face. But sometimes they can confuse or even offend the person you're talking to.

When using emojis, remember some simple **Dos** and **Don'ts**:

 Do have fun with emojis, sending lighthearted messages for friends to try to decode.

Don't try to have tough conversations with a friend using an emoji to soften the situation. Face-to-face is always a better way to talk so that feelings and intentions aren't misunderstood.

Do know what an emoji means before sending it to someone.

 Don't overload messages with emojis. Your BFF might love it, but your parents just want to know what time you need to be picked up from basketball practice.

 Do ask friends to translate emojis you don't understand so that you don't misread the message and feel upset for no reason.

*Finding the emoji message above too tricky to translate? Here's what it means: "Meet me tonight for pizza?"

nice or not?

Good manners make the world a nicer place—and that applies to the digital world, too. Give a thumbs-up or thumbs-down to the following posts to test your "netiquette" smarts.

1. Summer break is over. Can't wait to see my friends at school tomorrow!

PROVIDENCE MIDDLE

2. Yes! Studying paid off!

Math Quiz A+

3. Saturday Night Sister Sleepover!

4.

Great. Mom and Dad are fighting... again...

5.

Meggy B's concert was meh. And look what she's wearing! Did she check a mirror?

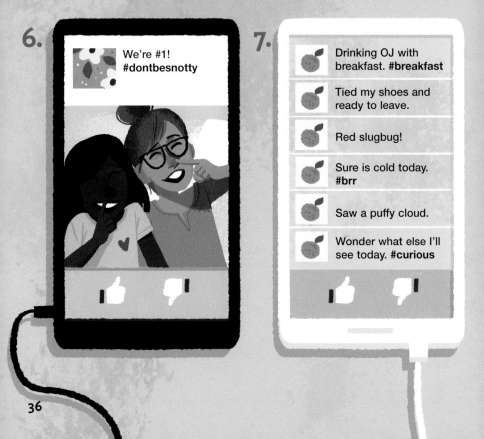

6.

We're #1! #dontbesnotty

7.

Drinking OJ with breakfast. **#breakfast**

Tied my shoes and ready to leave.

Red slugbug!

Sure is cold today. **#brr**

Saw a puffy cloud.

Wonder what else I'll see today. **#curious**

8.

Dexter got to do his fave things today: sit in the grass AND play with a tennis ball. **#happypuppy**

Answers

1. As always, be careful about personal info. Your house number could lead someone to where you live, and your school shirt shows exactly where you are going to be tomorrow. Never share clues about your location.

2. This post celebrates your hard work. So long as your name isn't visible and you're not bragging, it's OK to share the good news.

3. This happy post says that spending time with your sister is fun without sharing any personal info. It's guaranteed to make family and friends smile—and "like"! It's a real photo, though, so get permission from both your parent and your sister before posting.

4. What happens between your mom and dad (or any other people) is their business, not yours to share. If you need a friend to help you through a difficult time, it's better to talk in person or have a conversation on the phone so it's just the two of you.

5. Even celebrities' feelings can be hurt. If you wouldn't say something to a person in real life, then you shouldn't post it online.

6. Some pictures may seem funny at the time, but don't forget that digital images can stick around forever. You—and the person pictured with you—might not want those images to be around when you get to high school or start applying for colleges and jobs.

7. Posting every little detail of your life can cause readers to tune you out. Limit what you post to what others might find interesting.

8. The world can always use another adorable puppy pic!

steps in the right direction

Just like Hansel and Gretel left a trail of breadcrumbs in the forest, you leave a digital trail with your online activity. The only difference is that instead of getting eaten up by birds, your trail is here to stay.

Wondering why it matters? Safety is the first reason. But also, what you do online gives clues about the type of person you are to future coaches and teachers—not to mention a boss who might hire you for a job or a college deciding whether to accept you as a student. Smart steps now can be the first move in making your big dreams come true. Make sure your digital footprints create a path that leads in a positive direction.

Bake Sale!
Please sign up to donate treats for the PetsRSweet Charity Bake Sale!

You've got to hear this amazing little boy playing my new favorite song!

⚠️ Share with care

Before every digital step you take, pause for a moment and think about the possible outcomes. Will someone be sad, angry, or embarrassed by what you post? Can something you say be taken the wrong way? Will a picture you post shine a not-so-bright light on you, now or in the future? Considering the consequences now could save you trouble down the road.

friends without faces

It's amazing to me that if you post something on the Internet, it can be seen by people all over the world—even millions of people you don't know.

—Karen

friend or foe

With so many people on the Internet each day, there are oodles of chances to make friends who like, dislike, and follow the same things you do.

> Hey, MollyJK11 likes soccer and asiago cheese bagels, just like me!

But does that mean MollyJK11 would make a great offline BFF?

No. MollyJK11 is an anonymous profile. You can't tell if she is really an 11-year-old or even a "she" at all. MollyJK11 could be anyone.

That doesn't mean you can't have fun when you're online, though. It just means you need to be alert. Use this checklist whenever you're interacting with others online to stay on the safe side of friendship.

SAFE-FRIENDSHIP CHECKLIST

 Place the face. If you're not certain the profile is someone you know in real life, remember it could be *anyone*.

 Use only trusted, age-appropriate websites and apps where parents have helped you create an account.

 Always use an anonymous identity or profile, unless your parents say it's safe to be real.

 Never, ever agree to meet anyone from online that you don't already know in person. Tell a parent if someone invites you to get together offline, even if it's someone you think you know in real life.

 Trust your gut. If something seems strange, delete the request or leave the conversation, and tell an adult. It is not bad netiquette to ignore something that feels wrong.

Place the face. You've heard it over and over again, but that's only because it's so important: Never share personal information or details that describe the real you or your location.

digital drama

Drama, upset, and bullying don't happen only at school. They happen online, too—maybe even more so, because it's easier both to misunderstand and to be unkind when you aren't face-to-face with another girl.

Among friends

Maybe a girl wants a little attention. Maybe she feels hurt or mad at someone. Maybe she's bored and wants to stir up some excitement. Maybe it was an honest mistake. However a disagreement or drama starts, when it's online it can quickly get out of control.

One reason digital drama happens is that it feels more anonymous. You're more likely to exaggerate or say something you wouldn't say in person. Another reason is that in the digital world, your tone of voice, the look on your face, and your body language are all missing. Without these nonverbal cues, people can't see the whole picture.

To avoid or tame online drama among real-life friends . . .

Know the problem. It's easy to lose sight of what started the spat. Pause and figure out how you're feeling and why. Also, look back and see if a misunderstanding might have sent you off-track.

Take it offline! If you sense trouble brewing, it's time to tap, "Whoops, this isn't going the way I meant it to. Let's talk iin person!"

Don't go online in the first place. If it's a sensitive topic, talk it out face-to-face. Online might feel safer, but it's not. You need nonverbal cues to understand your friend, and you're more likely to be your true self if you're looking at her instead of a screen.

Drama with online-only friends

With online-only friends, take a break to get perspective and understand the situation. Then send a simple note to try to clear the air. "I'm sorry that didn't go so well. I like sharing soccer stories with you and hope we can keep doing that." If things aren't working out, it's OK to let this kind of friendship go.

Online bullies

Even though they're no fun, disagreements and misunderstandings are normal between friends. Bullying, however, is *not* normal. While physical pushing and shoving isn't possible online, a cyber-bully can . . .

embarrass you.

reveal your secrets.

put you down.

make fun of you.

spread gossip and rumors.

scare you.

How do you know it's bullying? Whether in person or online, bullies usually repeat their mean words and actions over and over again. They want to hurt or intimidate others. They want power and control. Being bullied feels bad, and it can leave a girl doubting herself and feeling helpless. A girl isn't powerless, though. There's actually a lot she can do.

Log off. Like walking away from a bad situation, just say "see ya" and sign off. Then block the sender so you stay out of reach.

Try being direct. If it feels safe, you can say, "I want you to stop spreading rumors about me" or "I don't like your teasing." But don't bully back, and don't be pulled into the bully's game. If she says, "Make me," respond, "I'm telling you to stop. That's all I need to say," and log off. The bullying may not stop, but you will feel more in charge of the situation.

Get help. If you've received a mean message, if you're being bothered repeatedly, or if you don't know how to handle an online situation, save the bullying remarks and talk to your parents or another trusted adult right away. They can help decide what the next step should be and keep you safe if they think you're in danger. This isn't being weak. It's standing up for yourself—and that's being strong.

Don't blame yourself. You may feel bad, ashamed, or embarrassed because of the bullying, but it's important to remember that it's the person who's bullying who has a problem—not you.

Take a break. It may take time and a lot of reporting for the bullying to come to an end. If it feels like too much to handle, take an online break and spend your time unplugged instead.

taking on trolls

If you like stories set in mythical lands, you may have come across a troll or two. Those folklore creatures are different from the trolls you'll find in online comments, though. Online trolls post remarks and questions that are meant to annoy, upset, and start fights with readers. Their comments might be related to a post, but sometimes they are random, just intended to suck people into their drama. If you come across an online troll,* take the advice of girls like you.

Don't take it seriously. If you know it isn't true, why focus on it?
—Sloane

People say things using technology that they wouldn't say in person. Don't take it personally.
—Carina

Block the person who is sending negative comments. If that doesn't work, save the evidence and tell an adult.
—Isabelle

Ignore it and don't make it any worse.
—Cara

Don't get wrapped up in the fighting and drama. Let it go.
—Desirae

*If you're seeing a lot of troll posts on a site, check the intended age to make sure the site is right for you.

44

speak up or scroll on?

Bullying? Trolling? Or people just kidding around? It can be tough to know when to stand up for someone or let it go. Answer these questions to find out if you should speak up or just keep scrolling.

1. You started following a new country singer online, watching her videos on the day she releases them. You're about to leave a comment on her latest song, telling her what a fan you are, when you see a long thread of people arguing in response to this comment: "Nobody likes country music. You should quit now."

2. Your brother's best friend always make jokes about how bad your brother's baseball cleats stink. You come across a picture of skunks posted with the caption, "Jake, I almost confused this with your shoes! Bwahahaha!"

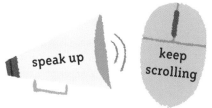

3. A shopping complex is being built in your town. A news story just announced that it may be built where you and your dad love to go hiking—your favorite spot! A debate in the comments breaks out, with some people saying the mall will bring in jobs while others see it as a bad environmental move.

speak up / keep scrolling

4. Your friend Lauren included you in an e-mail that she sent to your friend Claire, saying Claire was no longer invited to sit with you and Lauren at Friday's pep assembly. You know Lauren and Claire haven't been getting along much lately, but you feel stuck in the middle.

speak up / keep scrolling

SHOW YOUR SPIRIT!
FRIDAY 9:00AM IN THE GYM!

I just cut my hair and donated it!

5. Someone you only know online posted a picture of her new haircut. A lot of people commented saying it was cute and that it looked nice on her, but one person wrote, "Cutting your hair was a bad idea. Your face is too ugly and you need as much hair as possible to hide it."

speak up / keep scrolling

Answers

1. **keep scrolling** — When a troll is loose in the comments section, it's best to keep scrolling rather than get mixed up in the mess he or she is trying to stir up. You can still create a new comment instead of replying to the others, telling your favorite singer how much you enjoy her tunes. Just don't bother with the drama.

2. **keep scrolling** — Sounds like your brother and his friend are up to their usual antics. It's not uncommon for people online to make jokes and poke a little fun at one another. So long as both people find it funny, there's no need to speak up.

3. **your call** — Debating an important issue is not the same as having a fight with someone, though sometimes it can feel that way. There are multiple sides to every issue, and people will see pros and cons to each. If you have something to add, by all means, speak up! Your voice might help make a change. However, if you tend to take it personally when someone doesn't agree with you, scroll on to something more lighthearted. Videos of babies belly laughing, perhaps?

4. **speak up** — When two friends aren't getting along, you do not need to pick sides. But because Lauren included you in the e-mail, Claire may think you're against her, too. Respond to the e-mail letting them both know where you stand, and encourage them to work it out so that you can all be friends again.

5. **speak up** — Those mean words were intended to hurt, and that's never OK. You can speak up by telling your online friend to ignore the bully—and then ignore the bully yourself. You can also send a private message to this girl to see if she's OK. If you're not sure what to do, or if this keeps happening, ask a parent or another adult for help.

when virtual gets real

Remember how your digital footprint leaves a trail online of all the good things about you—your search for new crafting skills, the picture you posted while volunteering to clean up the park, and your sharing of a great music video? It can also include things that come back to haunt you in real life, such as . . .

a mean or sarcastic comment.

a casual text that gets misunderstood.

a post that employers or school admissions officers think is inappropriate.

a post that's embarrassing to you or some-one else.

The freedom you feel online can create a phony sense of bravery, making you say things you wouldn't consider saying face-to-face. Before you make it virtual—and virtually impossible to take back—do a reality check.

Rules of the digital road

Click with care.
Before you hit *send, post,* or any other button that will push your words and pics into the wide web world, pause first and think about the possible consequences.

Be word-wise.
Words and their meanings have a funny way of getting mixed up online. You meant to say one thing, and the next thing you know you've upset somebody. Read your words again before you send them on their way. Maybe use a clock and wait an hour. Or wait a whole day.

Slow your sharing speed.
If you post frequently, it's hard to give enough thought to a picture or post before you send it out, increasing the chance of a misstep. Also, you risk overwhelming or annoying friends and family with too many posts. Make yourself read it again, and ask yourself if it's really worth their time—and yours.

Think about others.
What you send, post, share, and comment on affects more than what people think about you. It affects your parents, siblings, and friends, too, when you make them the subject. Some things can be deleted, but they can't be unseen by anyone who's already read them. Don't share anyone's business but your own.

unplug and recharge

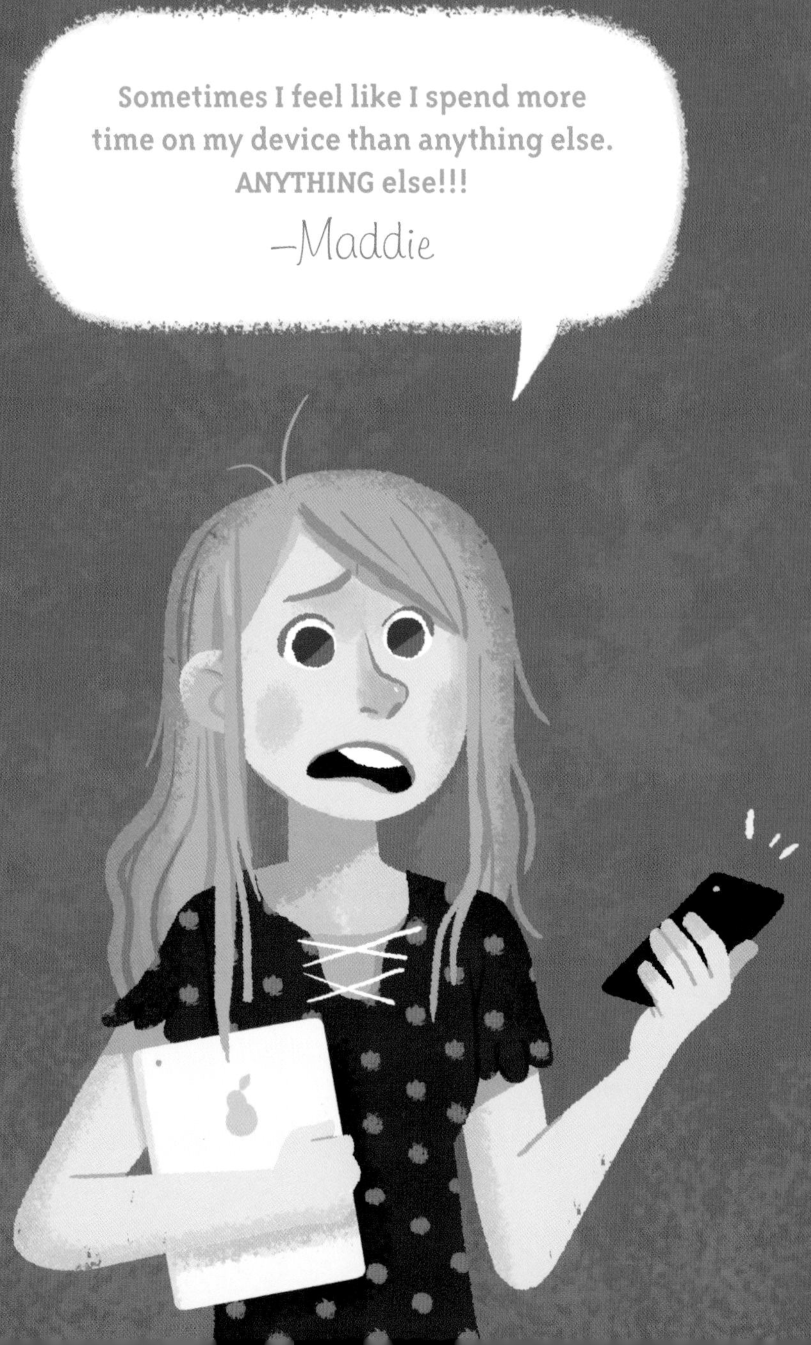

are you on autopilot?

Are gadgets making your life better?
Or are they getting the better of you?

1. It's Thursday, which means a new episode of your favorite TV show will be on tonight. You . . .

a. search online for a sweet and salty popcorn topping recipe to make while you watch.

b. send a group text to your friends to see who else is watching so that you can send messages about what happens during the commercial breaks.

c. settle in to watch all 12 episodes—and maybe move on to the next season!

2. You're down with a bug and can't go on the school camping trip this weekend. You . . .

a. stream a bunch of camp-based movies to watch while sipping hot cocoa on the couch.

b. respond to texts from friends wishing you well, asking them to send a picture or two taken by the campfire.

c. scour all the picture sites for recent posts, and text your friends for constant minute-by-minute updates.

3. Your three aunts are in town for a girls' shopping day in the city with you, your mom, and your sister. You . . .

a. search online for stores you'd like to visit and a place where you can grab a smoothie.

b. borrow your friend's selfie stick so that you can make sure every family member fits in your pictures.

c. snap and post pics of every moment of your trip—the three pairs of sneakers you liked, the hot dog cart on the corner, the fancy red car that zoomed down the street, your sister making funny faces . . .

4. Your music teacher Ms. Violetto assigns a group project. After exchanging e-mail addresses and phone numbers, you . . .

a. send out a message inviting everyone to your house for pizza and brainstorming.

b. ask your brother if he can teach you a few things about making a digital movie, and when he agrees, you suggest it to the group as a possible presentation idea.

c. start watching every online video you can find about the music you like and send each link—plus a few funny random ones— to the group in individual text messages.

5. Your dad surprises the family with tickets to an upcoming Saturday baseball game—your first professional one ever! You . . .

a. follow an online tutorial on how to craft a T-shirt that will show your team spirit at the game.

b. take photos in front of the stadium and in the ballpark, and then send them to your sister who's away at college—and one of the team's biggest fans.

c. spend the game posting pictures on the team's website, which the announcer said could be picked to display on the giant scoreboard screen.

Answers

If you selected **mostly a's,** you're in control of your connection to the real world. Technology helps you find activities to do with others, allows you to schedule when and where you get together, and entertains you when you have some downtime. As you get older, you may find you need to rely a little more on your gadgets to do daily tasks, but the good habits you have now will prevent the digital world from taking over.

If you selected **mostly b's,** you take some tech time-outs, but not many. Snapping and sharing photos, texting with friends, playing games, and learning how to make your own digital media can all be positive things, but only if you keep your screen time in check. Remember to take breaks and power down regularly, as well as swap out a few digital activities for real-life ones.

If you selected **mostly c's,** you're all gadgets, all the time. While technology offers great ways to stay in touch with friends, have fun, and get things done, it may be taking over. You may find yourself feeling edgy if your device isn't where you can check it any moment. It's time to find a better balance between real life and virtual life. You'll be happier, and your friends and family will be happier around you, because you'll feel more relaxed. And that makes connecting easier—for others and for you.

Start with small breaks. Have your parents help you make a plan and stick with it. For example, put the gadgets away for 30 minutes or so, and do something you enjoy. Ride your bike, walk your dog, play a game of Crazy Eights with your dad, fix a snack with your sister, pick out your outfit for the dance audition. Then build on those breaks. Slowly make them longer. Take them more often. Gradually increase your no-tech time each day until you stop feeling like something is missing when your device is stashed. It may take a little time, but the more time away, the better your mind and body will likely feel.

rewired

Did you know that American kids spend an average of seven hours a day in front of a screen? Gadgets themselves aren't bad, but you can overdo them, which can lead to bad habits. Take a healthy approach to screen time, and avoid letting tech time get the better of your brain and body.

There are tons of good reasons and ways to use gadgets. For starters . . .

Educational sites, apps, shows, and videos you can stream are great for learning.

Searching online for information about a subject for homework or a creative project of your own can boost your research skills.

Texting a thoughtful message can feel good for both you and the person who receives it.

Some video games can help you react faster when playing games in the real world.

Checking in with Mom or Dad is a good way to practice being responsible (sure to earn bonus points!).

Reading an e-book allows you to relax after a long day, share adventures with characters you love, and get inspired with ideas of your own.

But too much of a good thing can turn bad . . .

PING Your phone's buzzing with texts from a friend who found out her crush likes her back. And you keep getting pinged by your BFF inviting you to play a game. And a notice keeps flashing that your favorite video channel added a new episode. You can't think straight because your brain is starting to buzz even louder than your phone.

BZZZ Without seeing your sister's face or hearing her tone of voice, you think her message seems snippy. You decide she's mad, FOR NO GOOD REASON, which puts you in a cranky mood. Actually she meant nothing by it, but you've let it sap your spirit all afternoon—for no good reason.

DING You should be doing homework, but you decide to read just one more chapter in your e-book . . . and then send an e-mail to your aunt in Barcelona . . . and then watch a video montage of people falling in swimming pools. Before you know it, it's time for sleep, but you're nowhere near finished with your assignment. It's so easy to get distracted online and dig yourself into a hole.

BUZZZ The more you e-mail, text, and chat with friends and family, the less face-to-face time you have with them. Sometimes this feels like a good thing, but when you're at a friend's party or the school dance, it can feel like you've forgotten how to actually talk to people.

PING The first thing you do when you wake up and the last thing you do before bed is check your gadget. When you don't have it near you, you start to feel antsy. You can't explain it, but it's hard to focus, knowing people might be trying to reach you or are sharing things you can't see.

Too much screen time can leave you feeling stressed, overwhelmed, and moody. It can interfere with your ability to focus or sleep or make good grades. It can warp your perspective and get in the way of happy relationships with everyone around you. If your gadgets are taking over, it's time to unplug and give your brain a break.

finding balance

With a little awareness of your habits, it's easy to put the gadgets down. Here are a dozen big and little ways to balance your real and virtual worlds—and to inspire you to think of more.

1. **Play a different game.**
For every online game you play, pair up with friends or family for fun over a board game or card game.

2. **Leave it behind.**
For one week, choose times when you tend to be connected—the drive to gymnastics practice, the walk to school—and leave your phone behind. You might be surprised how free you feel!

3. **Nix multitasking.**
Stash your device when doing schoolwork, practicing the trumpet, or following a recipe. Trying to answer texts while doing anything that requires focus is hard on your brain, making you more likely to make mistakes.

4. **Start a photo album.**
Ask a parent to help you get your digital pictures printed. Then place them in a (real) photo album, and decorate the pages with scrapbook paper, stickers, and other crafty embellishments.

5. **Write a note.**
Using a pen and paper, write a note to drop in your friend's school locker or a letter to mail to your grandparents.

6. **Do some DIY.**
Find a project tutorial online, and follow the steps using real supplies. Pair up with a friend or sibling, and make it a joint project to create together.

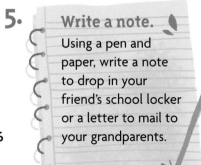

7. Snap a mental image.

Instead of using your camera to capture pictures of an experience, make a real memory that will always be stored in your brain—and with you whether or not your phone is charged. By living in the moment instead of looking for photo ops, you'll enjoy it more.

8. Listen up.

When you're hanging out with friends, put the phones away and be *with* them. You'll find your friend's gym class rope-climbing fiasco story a lot funnier if you're not scrolling through pictures at the same time. Plus, your friend will appreciate your full attention—even if you can't stop laughing.

9. Flip real pages.

Instead of swiping through pages in your e-reader, read a print book or magazine—especially if you're about to turn out the light for snooze time.

10. Don't answer.

You don't have to pounce on e-mails, texts, and comments the second they're received. Trying to be available all the time to everyone is exhausting and will only distract you from what you really need to get done.

11. Be social.

Make the table at mealtimes a no-gadget zone.

12. Power down

You need a good night's sleep. But if you're using a computer, TV, or device close to bedtime, the screen's light can flip a switch in your brain to "on" when it should be powering down. Finish homework that requires screen time earlier in the evening, and switch to offline projects an hour before you head to bed. Last: Make your bed another no-gadget zone!

posture perfect

Gadgets affect more than your brain. They can also be a pain—in the neck, the back, and lots of other parts of the body. That's because you use the same muscles for long periods of time, which is yet another good reason to take breaks. Another big reason is that people tend to slump and slouch while using computers and devices. Keeping your posture healthy will help keep you feeling good all over.

do THIS . . .

not THIS

do THIS . . .

not THIS

do THIS . . .

not THIS

hand it over

Holding your phone, swiping your screen, typing on a keyboard, clicking a mouse, and thumb-tapping text messages—your hands play an important role in your online life, so don't cramp their style.

Just like you'd do after running a mile in gym class, stretch your muscles if you've been on your gadget for a while. Here are some easy ways to give your wrists, fingers, and hands a hand.

shakedown

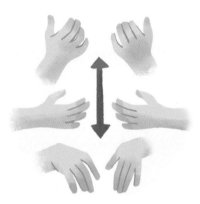

press on

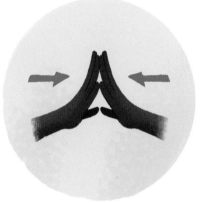

this way and that

open and shut

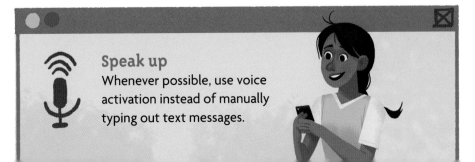

Speak up
Whenever possible, use voice activation instead of manually typing out text messages.

fresh air

Many gadgets are meant to move with your on-the-go life. Here are some ways to take tech outdoors for fresh-air fun with friends and family.

Backyard scavenger hunt

With a list found online or one you create, use your phone or tablet to look high and low for flowers, sticks, butterflies, nests, rocks, and more. Take a picture of each item, and race your friends or siblings to see who can complete the hunt in the fastest time.

It's a bird

Download a birding app to help you identify the feathered friends around your home, school, and other favorite outdoor spaces.

Green thumb

Learn what's blooming with a garden app that tells you the name of the flowers you see growing.

Stargazer

Ever wonder which constellations, planets, and stars are hanging out overhead each night? Use a sky map app to sharpen your astronomy skills.

On your mark

How much time does it take to sprint from your sidewalk to the garage or race around the block? Use a stopwatch app to test your speed, and make it a game to beat your time. When you reach your personal best, send a sweaty selfie to Dad letting him know the record you set—and challenging him to a race.

virtual you

I love all the things I can do with the phone, like videos and texts and even school stuff. But I also love to go outside and be with my friends and play with my dog. I try to have balance.

—Rosalie

new world netizen

With each digital step you take—playing games, sending texts, e-reading, sharing pictures, searching an online encyclopedia, posting comments—you learn more about the digital world, and more about *yourself*.

Tech gadgets and online activities can be part of everyday life as much or as little as you want them to be. Every girl is different. Get to know what feels right for *you*.

Whether you're online a lot or a little, safety is your number-one responsibility. You know that sharing personal information is the biggest no-no to being a smart digital citizen. And you know to think twice before you click, post, download, or send.